A Reply To The Report Of The Earl Of Durham

〚*Thomas Chandler Haliburton*〛

With an Introduction
by
A.G. Bailey

The Golden Dog Press
Ottawa - Canada
1976

© The Golden Dog Press, 1976

The Golden Dog Press gratefully acknowledges the assistance accorded to its publishing programme by The Ontario Arts Council and The Canada Council.

ISBN:978-0-919614-19-2

Printed in Canada

THE HISTORICAL SETTING
OF
HALIBURTON'S REPLY

Students of Canadian Literature have been inclined to pass lightly over Haliburton's political writings, especially, perhaps, his Reply to Lord Durham's Report, written at white heat and published in 1839, at first in the form of seven letters to the Times. Nevertheless its brevity and evident shortcomings should not deter those who may wish to attain to a deeper understanding, not only of one who is preeminent among early Canadian authors, but equally of the social and political forces by which both he and those who shared his Tory traditions were so fully shaped. Some critics have regarded him as the last of the exponents of Tory principles that had had their birth in the travail of the American War of Independence and the migration of so many thousands of Loyalist exiles in its aftermath; but, while this seems in the main true, it is nevertheless difficult to fit Haliburton into any neat category that may be devised because of the frequently contradictory character of his actions and utterances. To what influences this may be attributed is not always clear, unless it could be said that a recessive Yankee component, stemming from his father's background, may have on occasion, and unpredictably, obtruded itself upon the dominant Loyalist attitude deriving partly from the knowledge of his maternal grandmother's tragic death from shipwreck, starvation, and exposure, after seeking asylum in a new land beyond the reach of triumphant rebellion and its consequences.[1] Or alternately the psychoanalytic school of historians might find a propensity in him to refuse identification with the causes he held most dear, as seems to have been the case with another ambivalent literary figure, namely, Goldwin Smith.[2] Of course some students, including his biographer, V.L.O. Chittick, have attributed his evident inconsistencies to a self-seeking propensity, that is, to a recourse to expedients designed to secure his personal advantage. Born and reared in Windsor, Nova Scotia, a community possessing a class of persons who held landed estates, aspired to a condition of a rural gentry, sought for their children what education was afforded by the local Anglican and Tory college, he, nevertheless, on becoming a member of the provincial assembly for Annapolis, crossed swords on several noteworthy occasions with the Halifax oligarchy that had dominated the province since almost its earliest days. But if his plea for religious toleration for Catholics, his defence of the virtually non-sectarian Pictou Academy, his castigation of his own college as unacceptably restrictive, were designed to gain popularity with his constituents, they went a long way towards rendering him *persona non grata* with the politically powerful members of the very class to which he prided himself on belonging. These hardbitten and resourceful men were saved from having to strike him down by the death of his father on January 7, 1829, and the appointment of the son to the vacancy thus created on the bench, upon which he remained, first as judge of the court of common pleas and later of the supreme court, for the greater part of his active life.

Haliburton's opposition to the ruling Council of Twelve, however, it should be noted, was directed against particular measures, never against the existing structure of colonial government. With Joseph Howe he shared a common Tory tradition while an assemblyman, and it was only sometime after Howe's triumph over the oligarchy in the case of libel brought against him in 1835, and of Howe's subsequent search for a means to enlarge the area of colonial self-government, that the two men began to draw apart. The sharp comments and humorous gibes of *The Clockmaker* are directed, not against the form of government, but at the people of Nova Scotia for their slothfulness, lack of enterprise, and the seeming indifference to progress which Haliburton felt they exhibited. The artificial prosperity enjoyed by the province as a consequence of lavish expenditures during the Napoleonic Wars had instilled in the populace a habit of dependence upon imperial bounty which persisted into the more straitened times that followed, and from which it was Haliburton's intention to arouse his fellow provincials. Unlike Howe who came to see the solution, for a time in an elective upper house, but in due course, in some device for rendering the executive authority responsible to the people of the province, Haliburton failed to observe, blinded perhaps by prejudice, a connection between lack of initiative in the economic sphere and the prevailing system of government.

Colonial constitution-making had earlier reflected the belief in official British circles that the late lamented American war had resulted from too large a measure of freedom accorded the old seaboard colonies, so that they were determined to strengthen the executive branches at the expense of the popularly elected assemblies, by endowing the former with legislative as well as administrative powers, rendering them advisory to an appointed governor whose responsibility was to the home government rather than to the colonists themselves, and restricting assembly control of public revenues to narrow limits. In Prince Edward Island, where an assembly was already in existence before the end of the war, the situation soon became bedevilled—and remained that way for generations—by a system of absentee landlordism. In New Brunswick, where the population was overwhelmingly Loyalist, there nevertheless occurred at the outset a conflict between Saint John's Lower Cove people and the incipient oligarchy. A little later a more sustained agitation, led by James Glenie and Samuel Denny Lee Street, disturbed the province's serenity, but died down with the rise of the timber trade, only to be renewed in the eighteen-thirties when a series of reforms, including the separation of the councils, the Dissenter's Marriage Bill, and more particularly the securing of popular control over the revenues from the forest industries, eventuated in a state of comparative quiescence.[3] Unlike New Brunswick where many on both sides of the political fence were interested in timber, the conflict in Haliburton's own province was accentuated by the sharp cleavage between the farming and fishing populations of the outports and the commercial and banking oligarchy of Halifax. It is doubtful, however, that even here a crisis of a fundamental nature would have been so soon precipitated, leading to a revision in the system of colonial government, had it not been for the occurrence of the rebellions in Lower and Upper Canada in 1837, and the impact which these events had on imperial policy respecting the Maritime Provinces as well as the two Canadas. The significance of Haliburton's diatribes against the Earl of Durham can only be assessed in the light of that nobleman's analysis of the Canadian debâcle and the proposals which he offered as a cure.[4]

In this connection it must be observed that the constitution given Quebec under the Royal Proclamation of 7th October, 1763, had been a stopgap, and the Quebec Act of 1774 had been both a war measure and a belated attempt to do justice, as the authorities thought, to Britain's newly acquired French-speaking and Roman Catholic subjects in the province which they had set up under that name, and in the belief that these people would "to the end of time" constitute the overwhelming majority of its inhabitants. The Canada Act of 1791 passed as a renewal of war with France seemed impending, was thought of as a further measure of conciliation since the division of Quebec into two new provinces, that followed its passage, left the French in a majority in

Lower Canada and continued the protection of their religion, language, and social institutions as given under the Quebec Act. As the majority of Loyalists, who streamed northward into the St. Lawrence Valley at the end of the American war, found themselves by 1792 in the new province of Upper Canada, it was only the English bureaucrats and merchants, largely situated in the towns of Quebec and Montreal, who began almost immediately to experience the consequences of being an ethnic minority. Of course Pitt and Grenville, the chief architects of the Canada Act, were so caught up with a sense of the superiority of English institutions that they believed the French would soon come to recognize their life-giving qualities and demand reunion with Upper Canada, thus assuring assimilation to what these statesmen regarded as the exemplar of the higher form of western civilization. It was the failure of this expectation that eventuated in the rebellion in Lower Canada in 1837, and the Durham mission and Report.

It must be recalled, therefore, that the rivalry between the French and the English that had appeared at the birth of the Province, reached a minor crescendo in the dispute over the Gaols Bill in 1805 and during the so-called "reign of Terror" of Sir James Craig's governorship, became quiescent during the War of 1812, but immediately revived thereafter under Papineau's ascendency over the legislative assembly. The English mercantile class were now, what they had not been in the days of the Quebec Act, entrenched in the legislative and executive councils. Before long French, Catholic farmers, shop-keepers, and lawyers became locked in what seemed irreconcilable conflict with English protestant merchants over the control and disbursement of public funds, each dominant in one of the two branches of the legislature, each frustrating the interest of the other, the one favouring expenditures on roads and other local works, the other requiring canals for the improvement of the imperial trade-route of the St. Lawrence then in competition with New York's Hudson River highway to the interior.[3] It was not long before the mercantile class began to attack the French society of the seigneuries as an inert anachronism stultifying to progress as they understood the term. On the other hand the agrarian class, in defence of their position, soon seized upon the fundamental British principle involving popular control of the "purse-strings". What had begun as a clash between two Canadian interests thus gave rise to an assertion of popular rights unsanctioned by contemporary colonial usage, and denied at first by the imperial government. While they quashed the "anglicising" Union Bill in 1822 and offered Papineau's party control of all revenues raised in the province, in return for the provision of a Civil List, it proved to be unavailing. The extreme assertion of rights embodied in the Ninety-two Resolutions of 1834 constituted a clear forecast of the resort to arms that occurred three years later. In seeking to assess the validity of Durham's statement that he found in Lower Canada "two nations warring in the bosom of a single state", it must be born in mind that Papineau had never advocated rebellion and that, because of the presence of Anglophones in the ranks of the Reform Party, and in the leadership at St. Denis and St. Charles, a less simple finding may be called for. Where the ethnic conflict was lacking, as in the upper province, a similar constitutional defect, when coupled with religious controversy, the evils of the land-granting system, and other factors related thereto, fostered injustices of so severe a nature as to drive men into open rebellion. It was the existence of this constitutional anomaly which Haliburton refused to concede when confronted with Lord Durham's proposal for a system of executive responsibility in his Report on the troubled affairs of the Canadas.

Although it may be said that all of Haliburton's writings are political, construing that term in its widest sense, his specific observations and pronouncements are to be found in "The Bubbles of Canada", drafted at the instance of opponents of Lord Durham on the eve of the publication of his Report, and the "Reply" with which we are particularly concerned here. Both were published in 1839. To this must be added "Rule and Misrule of the English in America" which appeared in 1851, and speeches and addresses delivered in the United Kingdom towards the close of his life. While "Bubbles" was written in anticipation of what Durham was expected to say, the "Reply" was struck off with such haste that Haliburton accused Durham of making statements which, in fact, he did not make, notably a proposal for the confederation of the provinces which Durham had earlier entertained, but had abandoned at least for the time being. Some remarks are based on a misreading of history and the personalities involved, such as his comparison of Sir Francis Bond Head with Lord Durham, to the latter's disadvantage. Others are critical of his mild epithets in describing the rebels and their aims, of his strictures on Anglican near-monopoly of the clergy reserves in contrast to his praise of the Catholic clergy; but more than anything of his two most fundamental recommendations, namely for the union of Upper and Lower Canada, and the institution of responsible government with respect to all internal affairs which would, if implemented, have sounded the death knell of the old Tory oligarchies that had dominated all the provinces, with the qualified exception of Lower Canada, up to that time, as "Peter Pinder" stated in the course of his castigation of Haliburton on the latter's return to Nova Scotia following the publication of the "Reply".

It is curious, in the light of so many points of agreement between Durham and Haliburton, that the Nova Scotian author should have replied to the imperious proconsul in such a sustained fit of ill-temper, typical, however, in Chittick's words, of his "lifelong habit of embittered fault-findings on the losing side".[6] Undoubtedly Haliburton exhibited the characteristics of a variant personality; but he was also the heir to the Tory tradition exemplified by Joseph Stansbury and Jonathan Odell who had applied to the Whig cause and its leaders in the Revolutionary War the techniques that had been perfected by Charles Churchill and other satirists of the time. Haliburton made use of a different genre and employed novel literary devices, but he must have had some knowledge of the work of Odell who was a Loyalist celebrity, whose life overlapped with his own by twenty-two years, and who was a founder of New Brunswick and its capital city of Fredericton where his town house still stands.[7] However it seems wiser to regard Haliburton, who lived on into a new age, not as the last of the Tory writers, but as a transitional figure. Not only did he seem, later in life, to become inured to responsible government, and even an advocate of the Confederation of the provinces which he had earlier rejected, he caught something of the new vision of imperial federation which not long after his death was to be taken up by Joseph Chamberlain in the Mother Country, and in his own by such earnest publicists as George M. Grant and Sir George Parkin, although these two Canadians were possessed of an ethical component which, as far as one can see, Haliburton lacked. His political writings were nonetheless important as expressions of his most fundamental beliefs, and they contribute to a fuller understanding of his more exclusively literary works, embodying, as they do, ideas which once helped to shape the course of this country's development. Thus, as a reflection of the author's sensibility, the "Reply" to the Earl of Durham, together with kindred works, should be of some interest to the growing number of persons concerned with the study of Canadian intellectual history.

It is in this belief that Michael Gnarowski has undertaken to bring out the "Reply" for the first time, except for a photocopy, since its publication in 1839 in the heat of controversy.[8]

Alfred G. Bailey
Professor Emeritus of History
University of New Brunswick

Endnotes

(1) V.L.O. Chittick, *Thomas Chandler Haliburton, ("Sam Slick"), A Study in Provincial Toryism,* New York, 1966, p. 14.
(2) Alfred G. Bailey, *Culture and Nationality, Essays,* Carleton Library Series, No. 58, Ottawa 1972, p. 167.
(3) In New Brunswick the popular branch exercised control over important revenues through the device of a finance committee of the Assembly, a practice stemming from the old pre-Revolutionary seaboard colonies, the forerunners of United States congressional committees of later times. See W.S. MacNutt, *New Brunswick, A History, 1784-1807,* Toronto 1963, pp. 226-227.
(4) For what is in many ways still the best account of Durham, see Chester W. New, *Lord Durham, a Biography of John George Lampton, First Earl of Durham,* Oxford 1929, especially chapters XXII and XXIII.
(5) Donald Creighton gave classic expression to this theme in his *Commercial Empire of the St. Lawrence* (1937).
(6) Chittick, op. cit. 609-610. Among the points of agreement listed by Chittick were: Colonial Office ignorance of Canadian affairs; the need to open official careers in the imperial service to colonists; the desirability of making the French Canadians "British if not English"; that a strong British North America should be developed as a makeweight to United States power; but they differed as to the means of attaining these objects.
(7) On Odell, see Ray Palmer Baker, *A History of English Canadian Literature to the Confederation,* etc. Cambridge, Mass. (1920), pp, 27-30, 83. Also Moses Coit Tyler, *The Literary History of the American Revolution,* Two Volumes in One, New York 1970, Volume II, 98-129.
(8) Immediately following publication in the Times in the form of seven letters, *A Reply to the Report of the Earl of Durham* was published as a pamphlet by Samuel Bentley, Dorset Street, Fleet Street, London. Shortly afterwards a copy was struck off by a printer in Halifax. In 1972 the original was reproduced by microfilm-xerography by University Microfilms, a Xerox Company, Ann Arbor, Michigan.

A Reply to the Report of The Earl of Durham

Letter I

My Lord,

When your Lordship resigned the Government of Canada you were pleased to appeal to the people of the provinces and the American sympathizers against the injustice of the British Government. Since your return to this country you have appealed to the people of England against the injustice of the Colonial Governments. In the former case you complained, in most pathetic terms, of having been placed in a dangerous and difficult post, and basely abandoned by those whose cause you were upholding; of confidence withdrawn, powers withheld, and injustice committed. After having enumerated your wrongs, and declared the present Administration to be unworthy of such distinguished services as you were rendering them, you declared your independence and severed the connexion. At such a time the example was an edifying one, and afforded a pleasing proof of how much you had at heart the object of your mission, and how great a sacrifice of personal vanity you were willing to make in the service of the public. In the latter case you have attempted to show that the Colonial Governments are still worse than that of the Metropolitan State, and, imagining an analogy between the case of the disaffected and yourself, have argued, that when Colonists exceed the limits assigned to them they should be supported, and when their acts are unlawful they should be rendered legal; that subordinates have a right to assume the language of dictation to their superiors, and that, if restrained by force, it is natural for them to praise, as you have done, the neighbouring republic, to court its approbation, and declare their determination to dissolve the connexion. The tone and language of these two documents are, however, so different—the latter is so calm, so moderate, so totally exempt from vituperation, that I think I may congratulate your Lordship upon having recovered your former equanimity of mind. This, perhaps, may in part be owing to a difference in the political atmosphere of the two countries. The former was written in Canada, and addressed to a people labouring under a painful and unnatural excitement, and it was doubtless expedient and proper to use, in such a case, inflammatory language. By increasing the heat a fire is sooner made to exhaust itself. The latter is addressed to a phlegmatic people, and is sufficiently diluted to render the draught innocuous, although it has made it rather inconveniently large. In thus addressing your Lordship, I feel that it is unnecessary to preface my remarks with any apology. Your Lordship is an advocate of popular rights, and instead of confining your report, as humbler men would have done, to the Cabinet that employed you, you have decided upon publishing it to the world at large. It is true that that Report condemns without ceremony the conduct of individuals and public bodies in the Colonies; but we have been too long accustomed to hear constituted authorities treated with disrespect to consider this public dissemination of unsupported charges as inconsistent with the usages of civilized society. I feel, therefore, that your Lordship is the last person that will object to free discussion, and that as you, a mere stranger in the Colonies, and associated with strangers as your guides and travelling companions, have given us the benefit of your observations upon us, you will permit a Colonist to exercise a similar privilege, and to publish his opinion of you and your party. Your Lordship has designated every man that concurred in opinion with you as an able, intelligent, and respectable man; and they have returned the compliment, by applying similar laudatory terms to your Lordship, in those flattering addresses to which you have so frequently alluded in your Report. What sort of persons those were who differed with your Lordship, and who abstained from signing these acceptable testimonials, we are not informed; but as neither those who agreed nor those who disagreed with your opinions were ever admitted to your councils, it is to be presumed that no great value was attached to either, and that those persons whom your Lordship has thus condescended to praise have merited their approbation, not by their suggestions, but by their sagacity in permitting your Lordship to enjoy your own opinion, when they felt that expostulation is not only often useless, but frequently apt to convert vanity into obstinacy. That your Lordship was actuated by a sincere desire to promote what you conceived to be the prosperity of the colonies, it would be an act of gross injustice to deny; the zeal and the diligence with which you applied yourself to the task is deserving of all praise. Your Lordship's zeal has, however, not been directed by knowledge; preconceived opinions have not only led you into error, but have enabled others to impose upon you, and have induced you to prepare a Report which might have been compiled in England from public documents, and by a person who had never visited the Colonies at all. It is the production of a theorist, and not a practical man. That the bias of your Lordship's mind would naturally lead you to make such a report was well known before you arrived in America. It was expected by all parties. When your Lordship, therefore, states "that the discontented parties, and especially the Reformers of Upper Canada, look with considerable confidence to the result of your mission," you do them no more than justice. They have regarded it with confidence, and that they had good reason to do so is sufficiently proved by a general pardon which your Lordship was pleased to grant to those of their number who were found with arms in their hands, and the immediate return from Bermuda of those who had made such a formidable and murderous use of those arms.

This confidence however is, I fear, more creditable to their discernment than complimentary to your Lordship's wisdom. They were well aware that men who, in violation of their allegiance, had resorted to force to overthrow the Government, and had added murder and arson to the crime of rebellion, would not be stigmatized as "traitors" or "rebels," but would receive, in any Report that might be made on their conduct, the full benefit of that commiseration which the enlightenment of the age now bestows on such patriotic exertions, and that they would be designated by the milder and more appropriate term of "discontented parties." The result has justified their expectations. Your Lordship has also admitted with equal candour, "that you are well aware that many persons, both in the Colonies and at home, view the system you recommend with considerable alarm, *because they distrust the ulterior views of those by whom it was proposed to you.*" This, my Lord, is perfectly true; but it is not expressed with your usual accuracy of language. "Distrust" as little conveys the full force of their feeling as "discontented" does a correct idea of "rebels." These temperate terms were doubtless used from an amiable desire to avoid giving pain, but, as few persons will understand them in the sense used by your Lordship, it is necessary to speak plainly and to substitute intelligible language. We do not distrust their ultimate object—it has been too plainly avowed to admit of doubt; it is independence to be achieved by fire and sword. We view "the system proposed by your Lordship with great alarm, therefore, not because we distrust, but because we know the object of those by whom it was proposed to you, to be treasonable, and fear it will be successful." It would be in vain to follow your Lordship through the whole of the system you propose. I cannot reasonably expect that a public journal, which has so many other important interests to advocate, and has already devoted so much room to your Lordship's Report, will concede a similar space to my reply; I shall, therefore, confine myself to a consideration of a few of its most important parts. In my next I shall solicit your Lordship's attention to that part of the system which recommends a Legislative Union.

Letter II

Some of the changes recommended in your Lordship's Report are to be found in the communications of the Constitutional Society of Quebec and Montreal, of a date long anterior to your appointment; and your Lordship's omission of this fact is entitled to great credit, as your Lordship was doubtless aware that, if they were generally known to have emanated from so respectable and loyal a body of men, their popularity would have been greatly endangered among a certain class of politicians in this country. For this considerate act of kindness they ought to be, and I have no doubt they are, deeply grateful. It is undoubtedly a hazardous admission to make, but is rendered necessary, lest the British Parliament might suppose, from your ascribing all the system to the leaders of the rebellion, (whom you have so charitably and so condescendingly termed "the discontented party,") that these traitors were after all not very unreasonable people, but men whose impetuous temper had hurried them into the little imprudence, but manly error, of resorting to arms: but who, notwithstanding this venial offence, were really desirous of promoting some beneficial changes.

With such parts of the Report as are to be found in these documents I have nothing to do, but to express my regret that all your information had not been drawn from a source equally unexceptionable.

It is that part which is peculiarly your own, or was suggested by those able and intelligent men, the "discontented party," to which I object. Your Lordship recommends a Legislative Union of the Colonies, or a Congress for the whole, co-existent with, but superior to the Provincial Legislatures. This prescription you are pleased to think will, by its strong drastic powers, purge the body politic of all impurities, and not only effect a cure of all existing evils, however numerous, but however dissimilar they may be. The search after such a medicine, like that after the philosopher's stone, has long since been discontinued by enlightened men: but empirics still announce occasionally that they have succeeded, by accident or inspiration, where science has previously failed. So prone indeed are mankind to indulge in the marvellous, that these nostrums are always favourably received by the multitude, and their popularity is generally proportioned to their extravagant absurdity. This Legislative Assembly, which your Lordship recommends, is to be constructed after the model of the Congress of the

United States. Had your Lordship visited that country, of which you have undertaken to draw so flattering an account from the reports of the "able, intelligent, and impartial men of the discontented party," who have migrated thither, you might possibly have heard of collisions between the General Government and the State Governments,—of disputes about sovereignty and jurisdiction, and, of a term peculiar to America, of "nullification:" you might have heard of determined threats on one side, and fierce defiance on the other; of undefined rights, of constructive powers, and of unfortunate omissions. You would have learned that, though the people may petition the Congress, the Congress may not deliberate; that there may be rights unaccompanied by powers; and that written constitutions may be more vague and more uncertain than unwritten ones: you would have seen a Legislative Union of separate States, where the Supreme Legislature possessed too little power to answer the purposes of national government, and where the individual States had parted with too much to retain any separate influence or individual authority. In short, you would have everywhere beheld the melancholy spectacle of a Government unable to enforce obedience to its own laws, or respect for those of its neighbours; to protect its own armouries against its own people, or to restrain its own population from piratical incursions into adjoining countries, with which it had entered into solemn treaties of peace. But, supposing that your Lordship had passed through that country, as you unfortunately did through Canada, without hearing or seeing what other people had heard or seen, and had not learned that such was its condition, you would doubtless have inquired into the powers of the Congress, the imitation of which you so strongly recommend. Had you instituted such an inquiry, you would have found it had little or nothing to do; that though the separate States had conceded all the authority that could be safely intrusted to it, it did not amount to enough for vigorous action; and that, although they had rendered themselves powerless, they had not made the Central Legislature strong by their several contributions: you would have learned, among other things, that its chief duty was to deliberate upon all external matters; also to regulate the army and navy, the post-office, the coinage, the judiciary, the commerce with foreign nations, and the wild lands, not of the several States, but the domains belonging to the United States. Having acquired this information, you would naturally have asked yourself how similar powers could be committed to a Congress of the British Provinces.

Your Lordship has been more fortunate than most travellers, and has discovered many things of deep interest and great importance that nobody ever heard of before (so many, indeed, that I fear your account, accurate as it no doubt is, will share the fate of others of equal value, and have to await the confirmation of succeeding expeditions). But, notwithstanding, your Lordship's powers of observation, I doubt if you could find a provincial army and navy, for an object of legislation, or a coinage which they have not got and cannot have, or a post-office as a distinct and independent department. This latter, you must be well aware, is a part of the great general imperial post-office,—is connected with mails that traverse foreign countries, and packets that cross the seas, and officers residing out of their limits, and beyond their control, and in which the parent State has an equal interest with the Colonies. The supreme judicial establishment does not exist—is not required; and, what will doubtless have great weight with your Lordship, would not be popular. Their foreign trade they cannot regulate, so long as they are colonies, and ought not if they could. The wild lands are the appurtenances of each separate Colony, and there are no extra provincial domains that can be placed under its control. Where then are the powers of this legislature to be derived from? and what is it to do? Is it, like Congress, to be converted into a debating society, for wordy orators and vain boasting patriots? or a caucus for the election of the Governor-General? or a hall of pensioners, where demagogues are to receive eight dollars a day as the reward of successful intrigue? Where is it to meet? Are the French Canadians, the Papineaus, and the Vigers, to put on their snow-shoes, and travel through several hundred miles of trackless forest to Halifax? or are the "able, intelligent, and respectable projectors" of Nova Scotia to concede the post of honour to Quebec, to harness up their moose and rein deer, and speed over the untrodden snow to the capital? It is true there are no hotels on the road; but there would be not a few *ins* in the lakes; and such would be the harmony of these travelling legislators, that the *outs* would not quarrel for their places. Snug berths and warm berths are the objects of patriotic desire, and not cold ones. If sectional jealousies and local impediments create a difficulty as to the seat of government, as they did in the United States, where is it to be placed? Will you decide as those enlightened men did, and choose the geographical centre? If so, shall it be the small island in the Tamawaska Lake, in the heart of the forest, between the lower and upper provinces, or shall a more enlarged view prevail? Shall we regard the convenience of succeeding generations, and place it in the desert, midway between the Pacific and Atlantic? But I forget that your Lordship has solved the difficulty, and has promised us a railroad from Quebec to Halifax; and we make no doubt, when the great preliminary, but equally feasible, work of a bridge across the Atlantic shall be completed, that the other will be commenced without delay. It was a magnificent idea, and will afford a suitable conveyance for the illustrious members of the great British American Congress. I will, my Lord, not ask you where the means for this gigantic undertaking are to come from, because that is a mere matter of detail, and beneath the notice of a statesman of your Lordship's exalted rank. They will doubtless be had for the asking. The Government is liberal, and the Radicals will vote the money.

Letter III

It is difficult to reply to such a document as your Lordship's Report with becoming temper. It is so inaccurate in its statements of facts, so wild in its theories, so dangerous in its tendencies; it is so unsuitable to meet the public eye, so calculated to mislead the people of England, to irritate and alarm the Colonists, and to mystify and perplex what is in itself plain and intelligible, that I will venture to affirm the records of Parliament contain nothing so unworthy, nothing so mischievous. You have not only differed from all your predecessors,—many of whom were most able and distinguished men,—and the present and every former Administration, but you have differed also from yourself. This ought to have induced your Lordship to have distrusted your advisers, as it compels us to distrust you. The crafty manner in which Sir John Colborne's name is introduced, and the unhandsome insinuation that he was himself the author of these troubles, is so utterly unworthy of your Lordship, that I cannot believe it to have emanated from your own pen. It is evidently the work of an inferior mind, and as the document carries internal marks of being the joint production of several persons, I gladly avail myself of the supposition, to avoid the pain of charging it upon your Lordship. It was natural you should feel how immeasurably he is your superior; that while your imprudent manifesto invited one rebellion, his valour and conduct have suppressed two; and that in addition to the military laurels which you could not win, he is likely to merit those civic honours which you could and ought to have earned. You could not but feel, and feel acutely, that the whole tenour of his conduct, by its striking contrast to your own, affords a severe commentary upon your short and disastrous administration; but this, my Lord, is not his fault, but your own. All this I can easily conceive; but that your Lordship, smarting under these painful reflections, could have so far lost sight of what was due to yourself as well as to him, as to have given utterance to so mean and contemptible a paragraph as that to which you have unfortunately lent the sanction of your name, I cannot and will not believe. "Discontented men," my Lord, are not generally so respectable and intelligent as you give them credit to be; their counsels are dangerous, their association infectious. Your character has suffered by the contact. But if this was so unpardonable, what, my Lord, shall we say to the unkind and unprovoked attack you have made on Sir Francis Head? You have announced that you are yourself an injured man, that your feelings have been deeply wounded, and that you have not only been unsupported, but misrepresented. Could you feel no sympathy for him? Was there nothing in his case to awaken a generous emotion? Nothing to stay your hand when lifted to smite an unsuspecting and unarmed man? Were there none of those "able and respectable men" to suggest that his hands were tied, and that your gallantry could reap no honour in a contest where surprise, and not valour, should claim the victory? Your Lordship's opinion was not asked—you were not required to adjudicate upon his case; and if you had been, you were bound to have called upon him for his defence, before you pronounced judgment. *Audi alteram partem* is a maxim of which you claimed the benefit in your own case, and you should at least have dealt out that justice to others which you require to be meted to yourself. Had you done this, my Lord, he would have shown to you, as I know it is in his power to do, that you have been grossly imposed upon, and that you have unintentionally given to the world one of the most perverted statements of facts that has ever been published. He might, too, have suggested, that if an imprudent act of his, like that of your Lordship, had had a tendency to develope a rebellion, he did not desert his post in the moment of danger—having first increased the difficulties of his successor, and then insinuated things to tarnish his character,—but met his enemies in the field as became a brave man, and vanquished them. It is not possible, my Lord, that that part of the report which reflects upon those two distinguished officers, one of whom is absent, and the other disarmed, could have been written by yourself; but you owe it to your own character to disavow it, as well as other parts equally objectionable. The poisoned arrows discharged in this Parthian flight belong not to a British armoury, and whoever the auxiliaries were that used them, they were unworthy to be found in the train of an English Viceroy. Well might your Lordship inform the Liberals of Devonport that you had things to communicate that would astonish the people of England, for no man in it can rise from the perusal of this extraordinary document without the most unfeigned astonishment, the deepest regret, the most bitter disappointment.

In my last letter, my Lord, I had the honour to call your Lordship's attention to the inutility of a Legislative Union of the Colonies; permit me now to remark upon the difficulties to which it would give rise, and the danger to be apprehended from it. To give currency to this proposal, your Lordship has resorted to the sanction of his Royal Highness the late Duke of Kent. Your Lordship was wise in so doing; you could not have selected a name more respected and revered in the Colonies, where the memory of his condescension, his kindness, and munificence during his residence there, and the unvaried patronage of the Colonists after his return to Europe, will long be cherished with affectionate and grateful feelings. We have looked in vain for a patron since his lamented death, and the cold and chilly atmosphere of Downing-street forms a melancholy contrast with the genial influence of his paternal regard. He sought for talent and rewarded it, for loyalty and welcomed it, for merit and honoured it. Time did not impair his memory, nor distance his constancy. Where now shall we look, my Lord, for the fostering hand of power, or to whom can Colonists apply? We have neither votes to offer nor Parliamentary influence to give, and we require the countenance of those who are above the operation of either. Yes, my Lord, you were wise in affixing the stamp of that name, which appeals to our hearts, to this part of your document. It is gratifying to think that your opinions have undergone a change on this subject, and are more in accordance now than they were in the lifetime of that illustrious individual with those of a people who had ample means of judging of the powers of the mind and the qualities of the heart that distinguished his Royal Highness. It is true, my Lord, as you state, that the Duke of Kent, did institute inquiries on the subject; but you have omitted to add a most important fact, that those inquiries finally induced his Royal Highness to come to the conclusion that the scheme was visionary, expensive, and dangerous, and that he subsequently reject it altogether.

The plan which your Lordship now proposes was first seriously considered so long ago as the year 1757, long previously to the American rebellion; and, singular to say, after mature deliberation, was found open to so many objections, so dangerous to the rights of the mother country, and at the same time to the independence of the Colonies, that it was simultaneously rejected on both sides of the water. The pretended discoveries of Herschel of the movements of the inhabitants of the moon were so plausibly written that the greater part of mankind believed in their reality. The boldness of the assertions, and the minuteness of the details, imposed upon the credulity of superficial readers. No man had visited the moon, and therefore no one was qualified to contradict them. Your Lordship is in a position of similar advantage. You have described the United States, New Brunswick, and Nova Scotia, neither of which you have ever seen, with such discriminating nicety, that plausibility supplies the place of truth, and so few have ever been in those countries, that you may well challenge contradiction without fear of an opponent. The region where monkeys were seen without tails has not been visited by naturalists since the voyage of Lord Monboddo.

In my last I attempted to show your Lordship that powers similar to those exercised by Congress could not possibly be transferred to this new federal legislature: what power, then, can be assigned to it? All legislative functions are now enjoyed either by Parliament in its imperial capacity, or by the Colonial Assemblies as subservient to it. From whom will you abstract the power? If from Parliament, you cease to control these countries, and they become independent; if from the Local Legislatures, you annihilate them. This objection is a fatal one, and, as a practical man, I call upon your Lordship to refute it. But suppose the difficulty to be surmounted, the machinery to be constructed and put into operation, will no jealousy arise in the separate States that they are not equally represented; that the delegates of one by numbers, by superior talent, by intrigue, or by flattering addresses to a Viceroy, gain an undue share of influence; that duties are not equally levied, nor the revenue fairly distributed, nor public works equally undertaken in all? If a discontented demagogue should unfortunately obtain a majority in this assembly, where then are your Colonies? By gathering persons from all parts, you place them within the reach of contagion, and they return to their homes to spread the disease. Are the expenses of Local Governments not enough for modern jobbing, or must we add one of a more costly character because of a more exalted rank? If angry demagogues are to be appeased, or hungry patriots fed, who is to supply the means? The Colonists cannot, and I fear the Parliament will not do it. If your Lordship, one of the fathers of the Reform Bill—the advocate for retrenchment, the unsparing assailant of Tory profusion—if you, my Lord, even without a salary, and without a legislature to entertain, spent such an enormous sum of money in the short space of six months, as Governor of the Canadas alone, what, I may ask, would satisfy a man who makes less pretensions than your Lordship to loftiness of sentiment and purity of patriotism, who should have all British America, four millions of geographical miles, as the extent of his jurisdiction? The imperial magnificence of the Autocrat has dazzled your Lordship's mind, and led you to imagine an analogy where none subsists between the monarch of all the Russias and the Governor of a small and poor population, dispersed over the wilds of the American forest. The regal state exhibited by your Lordship will long be remembered in Canada. Though brief, it was brilliant. But, alas! my Lord, it is humiliating to think that the loss of a king is often less regretted than the cessation of his expenditure, and I grieve to say that much of the lamentation you heard at your departure arose from a source which is so little creditable to human nature. Even the sour sectarian, who had fondly hoped to have achieved the downfall of the Church through your Lordship's exertions, felt his cupidity stronger than his zeal, and with that familiarity of reference to sacred things that borders on profanity, and shocks us by its unnatural union of cant and levity, exclaimed in the words of Zophar—

"Though his Excellency mount up to the heavens, and his head reach unto the clouds, yet he shall perish for ever like his own dung. They which have seen him shall say Where is he?"

"He shall fly away as a dream, and shall not be found; yea, he shall be chased away as the vision of a night."

"The eye which saw him shall see him no more, neither shall his place any more behold him."

Letter IV

Experience teaches us that there are few things in this life so bad that they might not have been worse, though we very rarely find that a thing might have been worse had it not been quite so bad as it really is. Among the strange paradoxes presented by your Lordship's Report this is not the least. Had your facts been a little more accurate, and your theories a little less absurd, the tendency of your scheme would have been infinitely more dangerous; it would have been difficult to separate truth from error where they were so intimately blended, to define the limits of each, or to ascertain how much of the colouring was natural, and how much had arisen from infusion. A few drops of a powerful poison, though not discernible to the eye or the palate, will give a deadly effect to the draught, and yet leave the fluid to which it has been added as clear and pellucid as ever. Fortunately for the Colonists, this Report is so utterly vicious that it carries its own antidote, and presents less difficulty to an attempt to reply than to a selection of such parts as are worthy of an answer. It is overcharged, and, like Fieschi's machine, has exploded in the hands of the operator, missing the objects against whom it was directed, but doing infinite mischief to all within its reach, and to none more than the principal agent. Your Lordship has been pleased to draw a most flattering picture of the prosperity of the adjoining republic, of the tranquillity that pervades its population, of the effect of its institutions on the character of its people, and of the painful result of the contemplation of this scene of rural felicity on the minds of the Colonists, who are debarred from similar blessings. As a romance, my Lord, the production is not destitute of merit; the plot is well arranged, the language is above mediocrity, and it displays a fertile imagination; but as a state paper it is beneath criticism. May I ask your Lordship if you have ever been in the United States? or whether this is a sketch from nature, or what artists call a composition? From whom, then, did your Lordship derive this information that you have adopted as your own, and given as the result of experience acquired by personal inspection? Was it from those "able and intelligent men, the discontented party?" If so, my Lord, they lied:—excuse the word, my Lord, it is not in my vocabulary, and I am reluctant to use it; but men who have violated their oath of allegiance will prefer the word to "perjured," as you do "discontented" to that of "rebel". It is a milder term, it implies less atrocity, and is less likely to wound their sensitive feelings. It is a political synonyme, but it is more euphonous. "Discontented men" are apt, when excited, to use ferocious language; it is more dignified not to follow their example. "Mild words will turn away wrath." They misinformed your Lordship, then, which is still milder; for I observe your Lordship is careful of giving offence, except when you speak of the Church. The discretion exhibited in this respect is more conspicuous than the good taste, for there is little fear of goading the clergy to the use of arms. They do not desire incorporation, my Lord, with the States; they aim at nationality; they do not envy the Americans, but they hate the English. Did your Lordship hear it from the loyal population? If so, perhaps you could inform us what the objects of envy are. Is it protection for life and property? The Lynching of the South,—the assassinations of the West,—the forays of the East,—answer No. Is it legislative harmony? The Harrisburgh schism, the Hartford convention, the Carolina nullification, answer No. Is it exemption from taxation? The history of the celebrated tariff answers No. What, then, is the object of envy? I am a Colonist, and should like to be informed. What evidence have we of its existence? Was it in refusing with scorn their proffered aid to achieve their independence?—in the burning of the Caroline, or in the dispersion and slaughter of the Sympathizers? If such be the case, it must be admitted that we have a singular mode of expressing our admiration, and that a warm reception is an ambiguous term, susceptible of two very opposite interpretations. Your Lordship has doubtless heard of a certain speech appearing in the papers, which an orator had prepared for the press, but was prevented from uttering at the meeting for which it was designed; and this description of the state of America may possibly be a transcript of a tour in the United States, which your Lordship intended to have made, had not accidental circumstances required an immediate return to Europe. Had your Lordship entered the republican territories, which you say are more densely settled, and exhibit a more rapid growth than the adjoining province, you would have learned a fact of which you appear to be wholly uninformed—that when the United States were powerful enough to defy the whole might of England, to wrest from her an acknowledgement of independence, and to take a place among the nations of the earth, Upper Canada was a howling wilderness, the abode of savage herds of wild beasts, and the still more savage tribes of Indians. You would have ascertained, by a comparison of facts and dates, that since that period, though an inland province, possessing no port of its own, accessible only through one country inhabited by Frenchmen, and another by Americans, and receiving emigration, not like the United States from all the world, but solely from one nation, and from that one only in common with many other colonies, it exhibits, notwithstanding the unequal race, a growth not surpassed by anything in America or any other part of the globe. This Report is not your own, my Lord: your prejudices are strong, your politics are bad, and your credulity greater than either; but you are a man of honour and a man of truth. How culpable, then, is your negligence in signing this Report without due consideration! By affixing your signature to it you adopted it, and have made yourself answerable for its contents. In matters of business men suffer for such want of caution by losing their money, but in public life they lose reputation. Whoever it was that compiled this document, he evidently intended that it should produce political effects here, as well as in the Colonies, and the opportunity has not been lost to assail previous Administrations, to attack the Church through its provincial clergy, to advance the spread of democratic principles, and to enlist the sympathies of a certain class of politicians on the side of your Lordship. To effect this purpose, considerable adroitness has been displayed. The grand object was to attack the regular clergy (a subject of which I shall treat in a subsequent letter), but, to mask this, a fire is first opened on regular medical men and regular lawyers. Your Lordship is made to object that these men, who have first qualified in England, should be compelled in Canada to undergo a second preparatory course. Does your Lordship really think this a hardship? Is it, indeed, unfair? Exhibit, then, your sense of that injustice and a proof of your sincerity by introducing a law to admit colonial professional men to practise in England,—for a similar rule prevails here. Your Lordship was sent to redress the grievances of Colonists, and not of Englishmen, and we did not expect to find the list of our wrongs swelled by borrowing some of your own. They are everywhere considered two important professions,—the one having charge of your life, and the other of your property; and previous inquiries as to character are deemed as necessary as an examination into previous studies before candidates are admitted to practise. The decalogue, however, requires reform; it contains too many restrictions upon freedom, is inconveniently rigid, and should be modified to meet the liberal views of modern times. It is wisely rejected by the advocates of national education, and is a fit subject for a commission of inquiry. It cannot be denied that a very good lawyer may be a very bad man; nor is it confined to the professions; but the converse is equally true; and there are even instances on record where a very moral man has made a very indifferent governor.

Your Lordship has informed us, on the authority of a gentleman who passed rapidly through Nova Scotia, that his journey exhibited the melancholy spectacle "of half the tenements abandoned, and lands everywhere falling into decay;" and this fact is adduced to prove that the Government is so bad that the people are deserting the province, or abandoning themselves to hopeless apathy. A grosser misstatement it has never been my lot to peruse. It is not only not the case in Nova Scotia generally, but I know of no one district where the spectacle is exhibited, and few men know more of the Colony than I do. It is not merely untrue, but there is not a word of truth in it, and I cannot express the astonishment with which I read the statement. The only rational way of accounting for this extraordinary assertion is by supposing him to have fallen into one of those ludicrous mistakes that so constantly occur to strangers. In the first settlement of a farm, a rude and temporary building, constructed of logs of timber, is erected for the use of the family, which, as the proprietor's means increase and his arable lands are enlarged, is abandoned for a larger and more commodious framed house; and it sometimes occurs that this pleasing evidence of prosperity is found on the same property in the existence of both houses at the same time, though on sites at some distance from each other. If this supposition will not account for it, and it is by no means of such frequent occurrence as to warrant the belief, then we have but one alternative left us—to suppose that he has been grossly imposed upon, as your Lordship has, by listening too greedily to tales of wonder, and, by exhibiting too great a desire to gather complaints, to make out a case for your Lordship's theories of government. Let not this contradiction, my Lord, rest on anonymous assertions; there are landed proprietors here, and those who own no land, professional men and merchants, men of different rank and of different politics, from Nova Scotia, and I refer you to them all for a confutation of this slander. I refer you to the annual speeches of the Governors to the Assembly at the opening of successive sessions, and their replies, in which the prosperity of the country is alluded to as a source of congratulation, to the enlarged trade and increasing revenue, to every return, in short, and every state paper relative to the country that is to be found in the Colonial-office. What your informant means by lands falling into decay I do not exactly know; but, I suppose, he means that the lands are not so well cultivated as they were in former years. This, too, my Lord, is not true. Their system of agriculture is bad, as that of a poor people generally is; but it is much improved of late years, although a people who obtain the necessaries of life with so little labour as the Nova Scotians do, are not so easily stimulated to exertions as those of an older country, where the production of human food is with difficulty made to meet the demand. But, bad as their agriculture is, it is better than that of the State of Maine, to which you refer; better than that of Ireland, and, though greatly inferior to that of England or Scotland, quite equal to some that I have seen in both countries. There are few people, my Lord, fonder of a practical joke than the Nova Scotians, and the Viceroy's deputy was too good a subject not to be practised upon. How well they have succeeded I leave to your Lordship to decide. If his inquiries for "abandoned houses" were directed by a search after other things than truth, his eminent success entitles him to the credit of possessing some valuable qualities which you have omitted to enumerate among missionary virtues.

Your Lordship gravely tells us, that "there are in none of these Provinces any local bodies possessing authority to impose local assessments for the management of local affairs. To do this is the business of the Assembly." There are few things more difficult, my Lord, than to convey a denial of a fact in language that shall not be personally offensive, especially if the assertion of that fact be made in so reckless a manner as that which I have quoted. I assure your Lordship I feel the difficulty in its fullest extent, for, indignant as I am at such positive but erroneous statements, I am desirous to employ terms that shall embody that feeling with the fullest negative, and yet escape the imputation of grossness. I am a plain man, with all the rusticity of a colonist about me; and if my language is not courtly, you must attribute it to a provincial education. This statement, my Lord, is not true. Finding this to be the case in Lower Canada, you have, without inquiry and without scruple, asserted the same of all the Colonies. This practice is unfortunately not new; empirics always alarm a patient, by magnifying his danger, to induce him to follow their prescriptions. Had your Lordship called upon Lord Glenelg, he could have exhibited to you returns from every county in Nova Scotia, where "local bodies imposed local assessments for local purposes," and shown you how they were assessed, the manner they were collected, and the purposes to which they were applied. Nor is this the case in Nova Scotia only. But the foreground of a picture is the property of the artist, and a judicious introduction of groups of figures gives life and character to the landscape. The air of Downing-street, my Lord, is said to be narcotic, and the drowsiness of the people has long been the subject of much facetious comment. Happy, indeed, would it have been for your Lordship had you been subject to its influence, for then these incoherent dreams would have found a convenient shelter under your official somnambulism.

Letter V

It happens unfortunately that those persons who favour us with theories are seldom practical men, and that the result too frequently contradicts the prediction. That which is probable does not always happen, and that which ought to be a result, and that which occurs, are by no means identical. Hence your merchant regards with rational apprehension your political economist, and the practical statesman deprecates the adoption of the dreamy innovations of the theoretical politician. What succeeds in one country is frequently found to fail in another, and it is not sufficient that the machinery of government be perfect in its mechanism, but it must be adapted to the moral, intellectual, and political condition of the people who are to be subjected to its action. We have seen enough of rash innovation, of reckless change, and of dangerous experiments, of late years, to tamely submit to follow the prescriptions of speculative men like your Lordship. Mankind are the same everywhere, my Lord, and your Lordship's Parliamentary experience might have taught you that all legislators are more or less operated upon by passion, by prejudice, and interest, and that it is necessary to know the extent, the origin, and the direction of these influences, if we desire to bring our plans to a successful issue. But, though mankind are all alike actuated by these impulses, they are operated upon in various degrees, and by different objects in different countries. The prejudices of Europe are not the prejudices of America, nor are the prejudices of the Colonies identical with, though somewhat similar to, those of the United States. Overlooking or disregarding these obvious truths, your Lordship's schemes have been concocted according to the political creed of a certain democratic party in this country, whose favour it was necessary to conciliate, and although you have disregarded the feelings and wishes of the loyal Colonists, you have paid a reverential respect to those of the movement party in Great Britain. Of that party your Lordship may flatter yourself you are the leader, or, to use a more intelligible term, the precursor; but the very language of their invitation to your Lordship to accept this enviable situation conveyed so distinct an avowal of their having consulted only their own convenience in that offer, and that they valued your station and influence more than your talents or stability, that your Lordship very properly rejected, in the first instance, the proffered honour. It is deeply to be regretted that your pride had not overcome your craving after popularity, and induced you to adhere to a determination which would have compensated in character for whatever you might have lost in notoriety. Your Lordship talks of a Government of the Colonies, responsible to the people of the Colonies, and of a Governor ruling by heads of departments, amenable to the Legislature. However this theory may apply to Great Britain, it is sheer nonsense as regards a dependent state. Your Lordship has lost sight of the incidents of a Colonial dependence. The power of a Governor is a delegated power, and if it be designed that it shall have a useful and independent action, it must be held responsible to the authority only that delegated it, and not to the parties governed. He is an officer of the metropolitan State; if the control over him be relinquished, or transferred to the Assembly, then the Assembly is no longer subordinate but supreme, and he ceases to be an officer of Great Britain, and becomes an officer of a foreign country. If a Governor is to be controlled by his Council, and that Council amenable to the Assembly, then the Assembly controls the Governor, the character of its political relation is changed, and it is no longer a dependent but an independent state. Such doctrines, my Lord, so subversive of the supreme authority of the mother country, were never broached until the "discontented party" advanced these claims as precursors of rebellion. By adopting their views your Lordship has placed yourself in a very awkward dilemma. If you are sincere in the recommendations you have made, we must believe either that you are not aware of the consequences of your own schemes, or, if aware of them, that you have not dealt fairly, in not candidly placing the result before us, that we might know the extent and true character of the proposed changes. Physicians sometimes withhold from a patient a knowledge of the medicines they intend to use, lest the violence of their action might deter him from taking them, or the dread of suffering might be superadded to actual pain. In general it is both prudent and humane; but if the existence of the patient is to be endangered by the dose, the medical adviser is bound to state the risk, that he may decide whether he will incur the hazard, or bear with his disease.

Your Lordship is pleased to say that a Governor should conduct his administration by responsible heads of departments. This, my Lord, may tickle the ears of English Radicals, because it adopts the cant and phraseology of the sect, but such puerile twaddle can only excite the risibility of Colonists. Does your Lordship mean such heads of departments as the Minister of War, the Lords of the Admiralty, the Master of the Mint, the Chancellor of the Exchequer, the Minister for Foreign Affairs, the Secretary of the Dependencies, or the Postmaster-General? Of these they annually read a list in the English almanacs, but that is all they know of such responsible heads of departments; nor have they any officers whose titles or duties in any way correspond to such terms. The revenue of the Colonies is the great object of attention, as it is by that alone the resources of the country are developed, and works of internal improvement effected. This is collected by the Excise or the Custom-house Officers, and by them paid into the Treasury. In the Eastern Provinces (for Lower Canada is now without a Legislature) the accounts of those who collect and those who receive and disburse this money are audited by a joint committee of the Assembly and Council, the monies are voted by the Legislature, expended by Commissioners of their own recommendation, and drawn by warrants of the Governor, in most cases after the services are performed. What more of accountability, my Lord, would you have? The Treasurer, the Excise-officer, and their subordinates, give security for the faithful performance of their duties, are paid by the Legislature, and would be instantly removed upon any complaint of malversation in office. Is not this responsibility? The Custom-house Officers are appointed by the Board of Customs in London, and are under their control for this obvious reason, that it is their duty to enforce the Acts of the Imperial Parliament, and because they are Officers of Great Britain, and not of the Colony. Against them, I am happy to say, there are no complaints; but if there were, they are amenable to the Board that appoints them; and will your Lordship undertake to say that that Board would not entertain the complaints? If you are prepared to make this accusation against their justice, you must have received your facts from the same person who gathered the tales of the abandoned houses of Nova Scotia, for we know of no instances to warrant such an injurious suspicion. The Militia is commanded by the Governor, officered by people of the Colony, and regulated by temporary laws of the Local Legislature. Is this no control, my Lord? The road service is provided for by grants of money from the Assembly, expended under regulations made by themselves and by Commissioners of their own nomination, or else by statute labour, the accounts of which are audited by the Courts of Session. Is there no efficient control here? All township officers are amenable to the General Sessions of the Peace for the county, from whom they receive their appointment, and to whom they annually account. Is not this control sufficient? When your Lordship, therefore, talks of an officer ruling a province by means of responsible heads of departments, you speak of a state of things so inapplicable to a Colony, that it is perfectly unintelligible. As a theory this is, doubtless, very captivating; but as a practical measure it amounts to nonsense. By one of those strange inconsistencies that so disfigure this Report, and that can only be accounted for by supposing that there were several compilers employed upon it, your Lordship suddenly quits this train of concession to the "discontented party," and recommends that all money votes should first receive the Governor's assent before they are proposed in the Assembly. I will not enter into a consideration of the question, my Lord, whether this might not have originally been a wise measure, if adopted in the first American Legislatures, although I entertain very strong doubts about it, and rather incline to the belief, that with all the evils attendant upon the present mode, it is less objectionable than the other, but will ask whether it is possible that your Lordship can know so little of the feelings of Colonists upon this subject, as to suppose for a moment that they would submit to such a fundamental change in their privileges? If there is any one recommendation in the Report more than another that betrays a total want of knowledge of the feelings and prejudices of the people it is this, and no man but one who had never met a Provincial Legislature could entertain an idea that either persuasion or force could ever effect the change. As well, my Lord, might you attempt to force back Niagara, as the stream of public opinion on this subject. It is uniform, universal, irresistible. I do not wonder at this flagrant instance of ignorance, for it is natural; it was to be expected that you should fall into error; but I do wonder indeed, my Lord, at the coolness, the self-possession, nay, at the self-complacency, with which your Lordship discourses upon matters of which you know so little, and the vanity that leads you to suppose that that little qualifies you to frame constitutions, to demand their immediate adoption, and to treat with indifference or contempt the less presumptuous, but more solid information of others.

The exhilarating gas which your Lordship has inhaled, and caused others to imbibe, in the Colonies, has given rise to an extraordinary exhibition, in which grave and serious men have been so elated as to render themselves eminently ridiculous. Imagining their dimensions enlarged in proportion to their ideas, they have talked of a National Congress, international railroads, ship canals, responsible Governors, dignified heads of departments, representation in Parliament (for that, too, was promised to them), munificent Viceroys, imperial body-guards, and similar absurdities, until, like the frogs in the fable, they have well-nigh burst with the unnatural inflation. It is full time, my Lord, that this hallucination ceased, and that we recovered our senses, and set ourselves to work in the business of life like practical men. It is time that we rejected these delusions of a heated imagination, and called in prudent and experienced men to aid us with their advice.

There are evils in the Canadas that require prompt and firm treatment, and the constitutional societies of Quebec and Montreal, composed of men of character, property, influence, and tried loyalty—men who have given numerous and convincing proofs that they know how to defend their own rights and to respect yours, are the safest and surest guides. In the lower province we are better without your interference. "*Laissez nous faire*," was the prudent answer of the French merchants to speculative philanthropy like that of your Lordship. Be content to cauterize the diseased part, and leave that which is sound exempt from experiment. It has not yet been ascertained that it is necessary or advisable to physic a whole family because one member of it requires medicine. But if this theory is worthy of a trial, begin, my Lord, with your own. The experiment can be conducted under your own eyes, and if it should succeed, you may indulge the hope that these aberrations will not be hereditary.

Letter VI

The most redeeming part of your Lordship's Report is the zeal it displays in the cause of religion. The space devoted to this subject is so much larger than we had reason to expect, and so much greater than that allotted to your Chaplain on your outward voyage, that it has somewhat taken us by surprise. It was feared that "the still small voice" would not be so audibly heard amidst the din of arms, or listened to with such devout attention at the Court of the Viceroy, and I apprehend it may still be doubted whether it has found that favour so important a subject demanded. Manufacturers wisely suit the texture and quality of their wares to the taste of their customers, and the compilers of your Lordship's Report have not lost sight of this worldly maxim. Men of all shades of belief and of disbelief, except the Church, and of every gradation of politics, except Loyal Conservatives, have received their due share of commendation and encouragement. How is it, my Lord, that they have incurred your displeasure, and merited this rebuke? Have the Clergy, with ill-directed zeal, joined with the Premier in expressing "their surprise and regret" at your Lordship's disregard of their feelings in your official appointments, or have cold averted looks supplied the place of benedictions? Have your Lordship's compilers sought the opportunity to ingratiate themselves with the enemies of the Church here, by disseminating their favourite opinions under the sanction of your name, or did your unexpected return preclude your Lordship from calling upon the Clergy for their defence against these slanders? In this instance, as in most others, your Lordship has been too credulous and too hasty, but, like every ingenuous man, will rejoice, no doubt, in being corrected. Your Lordship commences by an eulogium upon the Catholic Clergy of Canada, extolling their exemplary lives, their loyalty, and many virtues. In this you do them no more than justice; they deserve this commendation, and I am happy to add my humble testimony in their favour. Had your Lordship's compilers exhibited in their Report any proof that they really valued these qualities, which they extol so highly, and expressed their approbation of other persons equally conspicuous for possessing them as the French Clergy, their impartiality would have proved their sincerity, and enhanced the value of their praise. As it is, I fear it was not so much designed for Canadian as for European circulation, for French edification as for Irish conciliation. Your Lordship next turns to the Dissenter, and alludes "to the position he occupies at home, and the long and painful struggle through which he has obtained the imperfect equality he now possesses," and again to "the strife from which he has so recently and imperfectly escaped." Whether this condition of equality in England be perfect or not, I do not stop to inquire; I merely ask your Lordship what this has to do with a Report on the state of Canada, and what other motive could have induced your compilers to introduce it, than a desire to make that Report acceptable to a part in this country, to pander to prejudice, and to add fresh fuel to the war of dissent against the Church, by enlisting sectarian sympathies against her? It is your Report, my Lord, and not the Colonial Dissenter, to which I object—I war with no man's creed: but if we appeal to England, let us appeal to its judgment, and not to its passions. Having thus attempted to conciliate favour by expressing your belief in their "imperfect equality" in England, your Lordship descants on the universality of the voluntary principle in America, and proclaims one of those discoveries that is to astonish the people of this country, not merely from its importance, but its novelty—that they have no Established Church in the United States. From this your Lordship argues there should be no Established Church in the Colonies, and then very wisely leaves your readers to draw any further inference they please as to England from "the *apparent* right which time and custom give to the maintenance of an ancient institution." Here your Lordship's spirit of conciliation departed, and having made up your mind to an assault upon the Church and the Clergy, you declare, as manfully as if you were resisting the rebels instead of that loyal and truly English body, "that you will not shrink from making known the light in which it has presented itself to your mind."

When you said "you would not shrink," my Lord, you evidently meant to convey the idea that you were about to do something unusual, something that would deter ordinary men, and required an exercise of moral courage. The word was appropriate. Most men would revolt at the idea of presenting an *ex parte* statement, would shudder at the thought of doing an act of injustice, and shrink from an attempt to alienate the affections of a people from their Clergy. Most men, my Lord, on meeting in the wilds of America with an English clergyman would have been touched with far different feelings from those which appear to have affected your Lordship. Is it nothing to leave the home of his fathers, the friends of his youth, and the refinements of life, to encounter privation and toil in a foreign land in the service of his Master? Was there nothing in the mutual recollections of your common country to call up a sympathy for his exile, or awaken a respect for his sacrifice? Could you listen to his ministrations, to the well-known liturgy of your own Church, the prayers of your youth, and the devotion of your riper years, so far from home, without emotion? My Lord, I envy you not the nerve that enables you, "without shrinking," to represent these services as unsuited to the country, to state your preference of casual, uncertain, and irregular missionary visits, to the regular, stated, and certain offices of the Church; to exalt all other sects over it; to awaken the prejudice of all against it; and to recommend the division of its property among other denominations. When you first began to feel a preference for itinerancy, which, in the beautiful language of Scripture, "Leaveth her eggs in the earth, and warmeth them in dust; and forgetteth that the foot may crush them, or that the wild beast may break them," did you ask the clergy to solve your doubts? Did you inquire whether the Church had its missionary as well as its parochial clergy, or whether they did not frequently unite the labours of both? Had you done so, my Lord—had you read the affecting reports of these faithful and zealous men, you would have found abundant evidence that the Church visiting Missionary in a new country is the pioneer of a stationary ministry—"The voice of one crying in the wilderness, prepare ye the way of the Lord,"—that he is found on the outskirts of civilization, where he clears the field and sows the seed, and, advancing with the march of migration, leaves his appointed fellow-labourer to garner up the harvest in the house of the Lord. When you extol the benefits of a French priest to a French community, how could your Lordship assert that an English Clergyman conferred no benefits on an English congregation, when you everywhere found the flock of one disobedient to their pastor and traitorous to their Queen, while the great body of the parishioners of the other afforded the pleasing contrast of respect for the laws and fidelity to their Sovereign? With this fact before you, now notorious to all mankind, your Lordship has been made, by your disingenuous compilers, to peril your character by asserting, "I know of no parochial clergy in the world whose zealous discharge of their clerical duties has been productive of more beneficial consequences than the French Canadians." I know of none, my Lord, who are more zealous, more exemplary, or more deserving of praise, but I know of none who have been more signally and deplorably unsuccessful. When your Lordship speaks with complacency of their tithes, of their having been retarded in their labours from want of means, and of the policy of a better provision for them in future, had you no remorse of conscience when you assailed your own Church, represented it as having too much of the public money, as comprising none but the opulent, and lauded the policy of stripping it of its lands, to appease the craving appetite of others? More just, my Lord, as well as more generous, than those who cast lots for "the garment without a seam," you consent that it shall be rent to pieces, and distributed to each according to his necessities. Not content with making your Lordship appear in the unamiable light of acting unfriendly; your compilers have represented you as willing to act unfairly. You are made to say, when speaking of the Church Clergyman, "though he 'may' have no right to levy tithes, for even this has been made a question, he is," &c. The evident intent of this artfully-worded clause, that dares to hint, but fears to assert, was to insinuate that a question exists in Upper Canada as to the right of levying tithes, and to convey an idea that your Lordship does not concur in the claim. If such were not the case, the misstatement would be superfluous, and your compilers are too acute and too subtle to hazard such assertions unnecessarily.

Can it be believed, my Lord, by those who value truth, that your coadjutors in preparing this Report were not actuated by a malignant spirit of misrepresentation, when they are informed that a law exists to remove all doubts from jealous and rival sects upon this subject, renouncing all claims to such a right and precluding slander from even insinuating the desire for an impost, when the power to levy it, if it had a legal existence, was annihilated for ever? Why, I may ask, was this ambiguous and deceptive clause introduced at all? and if there be sufficient reason for its introduction, why was it not accompanied by the explanation I have just given? The cause, my Lord, is obvious: the word "tithe" is too familiar a topic with agitators not to be connected on every occasion with the Church, and if the declaratory act were to be mentioned, it would be impossible to conceal the still more important fact that the seventh of land, or the clergy reserve, was given in lieu of tithes; that the Church was otherwise provided for, and it was deemed proper it should not have two endowments of so extensive a description. On the argument against the policy of establishing a dominant Church in the Colonies, where not only none exists, but where no one that I have ever met advocates its introduction, and on the insidious application of the word "dominant" to the Church of England, as now constituted in the provinces, I shall not comment. I conceive it to be addressed rather to the movement party of this country than to the Legislature or the Government. I cannot believe that your Lordship was aware of those injurious aspersions when you signed the Report, but it was your duty, my Lord, to have examined it minutely before you adopted it. The publisher is held responsible in law as well as the author. Such things may be popular, but they are not respectable. Gross food like this, my Lord, excites but never satisfies the appetite of the populace, and he who ministers to its wants will soon find that he fills both a dangerous and a thankless office.

Letter VII

A great observer of human nature has informed us, that misery derives consolation from having associates in the same unhappy condition with itself; but he has omitted to notice the propensity inherent in us to implicate others in our troubles for the sake of their agreeable fellowship. That your Lordship should desire the company of Sir John Colborne in the political shipwreck you have encountered was, therefore, quite natural, and your compilers have endeavoured to make him a fellow-passenger and joint sufferer, that you might not be deprived of the comfort arising from condolence. "The last public act," say these ingenuous and liberal men, "of Sir John Colborne before quitting the Province in 1835, the establishment of fifty-seven Rectories, has completely changed the aspect of the question. In the opinion of many persons, this was the chief predisposing cause of the recent insurrection." Had your Lordship been content with having this distinguished but criminal man arraigned at the bar of public opinion with yourself, you would have doubtless succeeded; but, in your indiscreet haste to secure other persons, you have loosened your hold of him, and suffered him to escape. This is much to be regretted, for, by distracting attention and dividing responsibility, your own position would have been less painful as well as less perilous. Your compilers were desirous of involving the Law Officers of the Crown in their indictment, in the hope, no doubt, that legal ingenuity would discover one of those numerous devices by which the guilty so often escape. "Last summer," continue these agreeable and conciliatory gentlemen the compilers of this ponderous Report, "the controversy was revived with more heat than ever by the most inopportune arrival in the Colony of opinions given by the English Law Officers in favour of the legality of the establishment of the Rectories."

In another part we are informed that Sir Francis Head "entrapped them into rebellion;" we now learn that Sir John Colborne baited this ingenious instrument, the rebel trap, with a Rectory. Sir John Colborne then provoked an insurrection by defining the limits of parishes, in obedience to the law of the land! But this is absurd. Then it must have been the Law Officers that gave the opinion who were to blame, not for giving an unsound opinion, for that is not questioned, but for giving it "inopportunely." Here again is disclosed one of those recondite discoveries that was to astonish mankind, and the parturition of the mountain has rewarded us with this secret in return for our anxious attendance upon it during a trying and protracted period of gestation.

Had your Lordship seen as much of the American forests as I have, you would have learned that a man who loses himself in those interminable wilds generally travels in a circle, and after exhausting his strength and his spirits, has the mortification to find himself on the same spot from which he started. Your Lordship is in a similar situation of distress in your bewildered search after "the predisposing cause of the rebellion." You commenced with the Church, and successively encountering Sir John Colborne, the Rectories, the Law Officers of the Crown, and Sir Francis Head, returned, after great toil, to the Church again. Common humanity, my Lord, requires that we should put a man in the right road who has lost his way, and if you will give me permission, I will undertake to perform this friendly office. "The predisposing cause" of the first rebellion is to be sought for much nearer home than your Lordship is aware of, and it was unnecessary for you to traverse the seas, at such great inconvenience to yourself, and such enormous expense to the nation, to institute these interesting and laborious investigations. It consisted in a correspondence carried on in London by persons of influence and political station with certain "intelligent, able, and respectable men" of "the discontented party" in Canada, in which the mild, liberal, and paternal Government of the parent State was called "a baneful domination," and in which they were advised "to resist the Parliament," to agitate continually, and to keep constantly before their eyes "the glorious example of the United States." This advice was followed by promises of Parliamentary support which should sanction their conduct and embarrass the Government, and a certain portion of the press, conducted by "intelligent, able, and respectable men" of the "discontented party" here, by disseminating the grossest mis-statements and calumnies of the local authorities, led them to believe that they had the ability as well as the disposition to render them valuable assistance in their patriotic endeavours. Prompted by this advice, and relying on these promises, the "discontented party," who had nothing to lose, and everything to gain by a revolution, boldly followed their instructions, and drew the sword.

This, my Lord, was the "predisposing cause" of the first outbreak; the second found "a predisposing cause" in a certain imprudent, ill-judged, and inflammatory proclamation issued by a certain Governor-General, in which he accused the Government that employed him, of all that the rebels had accused it; complained that Parliament legislated in ignorance and indifference on Canadian matters, and declared that, as a man of honour, he could no longer continue to hold office under it. This "able and intelligent," but "discontented man," repeated, "without shrinking," this edifying language before the delegates of the other Colonies in a manner so touching as to draw tears from the eyes of those who listened to the affecting catalogue of his wrongs, and at a military festival, which of all places was the most appropriate for such a recital, as it is the special duty of soldiers to canvass the orders of their superiors, he adverted in strong language to the same topics. A Lord High Commissioner defying and denouncing his Government to the rebels he was sent to quell, informing the exiles that no impediment existed to their return, and abandoning his post when his presence was most needed, was a predisposing cause to others to follow such a laudable example. Few people are so fortunate as to have such an instructive lesson read to them by such high authority.

From this sketch, my Lord, you will perceive that the Church, which enjoins on its members "to be obedient to those in authority," to "honour the King," and to "render to Caesar the things that are Caesar's," could not by any possibility be a predisposing cause to rebellion. I think also that your Lordship will concur in opinion with me, that, if the statement I have just submitted to you be true, both those men who were "the predisposing cause" of the first, and the man who was "the predisposing cause" of the second rebellion, ought to be impeached, and that whatever a reformed Parliament may do, no doubt can exist that an unreformed Parliament, such as once existed in this country, would have lost no time in visiting those men with that punishment which such serious offences so justly merited.

Having now set your Lordship right, I am anxious to give you some directions that will enable you to avoid a similar mistake in future. Should your Lordship unfortunately hear of a third insurrectionary movement, you will find "the predisposing cause" in a certain Report, which certain persons unknown have recently compiled, and very properly published, and from its republican tone as properly addressed to the Queen, in which they, the said compilers, "not having the fear of God before their eyes, but listening to the instigations of the Devil, have wickedly, craftily, and of malice aforethought," deceived your Lordship's unsuspecting confidence, misstated facts,* and misrepresented motives, and to divert attention from the real offenders, who travel under the assumed name of "discontented gentlemen," have raised "a hue and cry" against the Government of the Queen and the Church of God.

By following these directions, your Lordship will be able to extricate yourself from the labyrinth of crooked paths into which your compilers have so insidiously and designedly conducted you, and to arrive at the object of your anxious search—"the predisposing cause of the rebellion."

Confiscation of property was once a consequence of treason, before a reform of our criminal code reduced the offence in the scale of guilt, and applied to that crime the mitigated name of "discontent," but I am not aware that it was ever resorted to in any age as a punishment for loyalty. To pardon the guilty and punish the innocent is a modern theory, and being first promulgated in this Report is doubtless one of those discoveries so loudly proclaimed at Devonport as likely to create universal astonishment. Your compilers make you to say, "I know of no mode of giving satisfaction but by repealing all provisions in Imperial Acts that relate to the application of the Clergy reserves and the funds arising from them." Ignorant of the world, and holding the antiquated notions of Colonial simplicity, I should have thought, my Lord, it was your duty to have inquired into the right of the Church to this property, and if you found upon such investigation that it belonged to the Church, to state with that frankness and manliness that becomes a Peer of the Realm, and "*without*

---

*As most of the misstatements exposed in these letters refer to matters in the Colonies, it may be as well to select a few immediately within the knowledge of the people of this country, that they may see how little dependence is to be placed on the accuracy of any part of the Report. His Lordship inserts a complaint that, although the proper height according to law is preserved between the decks of emigrant ships, the officers do not enforce the measurement between the beams. Now, it appears that the power of the officers extends to the height between the *decks*, but not between the *beams*, of which the complaint is made. He next points out the ignorance of the surgeons of emigrant ships, when the ignorance consists in supposing surgeons are required by law in vessels sailing to America. He also inserts a remark relative to selecting ships which are scarcely sea-worthy, when, in fact, the officers are not empowered by law to select the ships at all: yet upon such grounds as these was his Lordship made by his compilers to prefer a sweeping charge of neglect of duty, upon the worthy superintendant of this department, and eleven or twelve meritorious officers of the navy who honestly discharge their functions at their respective stations. Almost every part of the Report teems with similar errors, betraying deplorable ignorance and most inexcusable carelessness in the compilers.

shrinking," that the first duty of a Government being to protect people in the enjoyment of their property, these reserves must be held sacred from all interference, and that, so far from countenancing such sacrilegious plunder, you would resist it to the utmost of your power; and on the other hand, if it did not belong to the Church, that it was equally your duty to deliberate upon the mode of its distribution that should be best calculated to promote the cause of true religion. I should have thought, that instead of embodying rumours as facts, and pretensions as truths, your Lordship, from the illegality of your first measures, distrustful of your own judgment on matters of law, would have called for legal opinions, and especially would have requested a perusal of that given by so distinguished a man as Mr. Justice Patteson on this subject. I should have thought it your duty to have stated to those claimants, among other proofs of the Clergy of the Church of England being the parties to whom this property belonged, these remarkable words of this learned judge—"I have no doubt that the Clergy of the Church of England are that body: I am also of opinion that the Governors of the Provinces, acting under His Majesty's direction, cannot legally make any appropriation to others;" and thus allayed irritation by showing its injustice, and suppressed agitation by exhibiting its folly as well as its inutility. But such opinions I find are long since exploded as too primitive for this enlightened age, when Reform has enlarged our ideas as well as extended our Suffrage. I shall not here enter into any particulars of this title—it is not the place for such discussions. They would distract attention and occupy more space than a public journal can devote to them; nor shall I inquire whether this provision was a wise one, or a convenient one, or whether an arrangement could not be made satisfactory to all and injurious to none. It is the principle to which I object, that the property of any individual or any body of men should be forcibly taken from them, and distributed among others to appease their turbulent clamours. Your Lordship is entitled to the credit of great liberality, but has no pretension to the honour of originality in propounding this doctrine. History is full of instruction on this subject, and he who will not draw the moral deserves to suffer for his obstinate refusal. In this country it has already been announced as an article of the political creed of a certain party, and will doubtless receive additional weight from the sanction of your Lordship's name. But, my Lord, in the eventful changes that are in progress, and which I fear a chastening Providence has in store for us, the division of the Lambton Estates may awaken your Lordship when too late to a knowledge of this truth, that the principles of justice are uniform, universal, and immutable, and that that which is right in Canada cannot by any possibility be wrong in England.

I am now about to take my leave of you, my Lord, for ever: circumstances over which I can exercise no control, but which at this juncture I deeply deplore, render it necessary that I should close these remarks upon your Lordship's Report. There are other subjects of great importance that require explanation, but I must leave that task to others. Having done my duty, I shall await the result as becomes a good subject, with a full reliance upon the justice of that tribunal to which the matter is referred. If there are any parts of these letters calculated to give your Lordship pain, believe me, the infliction has been mutual. If I have expressed myself strongly, it is because I feel deeply, and not because I harbour any of those base propensities, now so common in Great Britain, to impair the respect that is due to rank and station. Such a motive would be as unworthy as the servile adulation you have received is mean and contemptible. The nobility of this country give stability to the Government, splendour to the Throne, dignity to the Legislature, and character to the People, and are at once its brightest ornament and its best support. When your Lordship shall have occupied the high station a few years longer to which you have been so recently elevated, and the pride of rank shall have departed with its novelty, and when the exercise of new duties shall have superseded former habits of agitation, I make no doubt that better, calmer, and juster notions will prevail in your Lordship's mind.

The Crown and the People have an equal claim upon the protection of the Peers against any encroachments on their rights, and they best consult their own safety in a vigilant restraint of both within their legitimate spheres. An undue preponderance given to the one endangers the liberty of the subject; an opposite inclination of power perils the safety of the Sovereign; but vibration affects the harmonious action of each, and, disturbing the balance of the constitution, produces a cessation of its powers. This crisis, my Lord, is called a revolution. Similar causes produce similar effects. The Report of La Fayette, on his return from the States, subverted monarchy in France; the Report of your Lordship, equally laudatory of that Republic and its institutions, is no less dangerous from its democratic tendencies to the Monarchy of England. Let us hope, that as your Lordship is as much superior to that man in principle as you are fortunately inferior to him in talent, there may be no resemblance in the result, and that the crude and undigested theories of a few visionary men will not be substituted for the experience of ages.

I have the honour to be,
Your Lordship's most obedient servant,
A COLONIST

The End.

www.ingramcontent.com/pod-product-compliance
Lightning Source LLC
Chambersburg PA
CBHW030306030426
42337CB00012B/614